The

Incomprehensible

The Unspoken words

Piyush Chaudhari

BookLeaf
Publishing

India | USA | UK

"To my parents, my brother, and God, who gave me the gift of dreams and the ability to realize them"

Acknowledgment

Dear Readers,

Poetry has been woven into human culture since the earliest records of history. Sometimes, I wonder if poetry might have been the first art form practiced by humankind—emerging soon after the development of language itself. In India, we have a rich tradition of oral hymns passed down through generations, preserving history and emotion through spoken word.

A poem is more than just a crafted work; it is a conversation between the poet and the reader or listener, a shared space where thoughts and feelings intersect. In this collection, each poem touches upon a unique challenge, emotion, situation, or reflection. Although I may not fully understand the impulse behind each piece, I hope these lines offer you something to connect with, something that resonates, and perhaps even something to hold onto. The poems that I have written are not of a single genre. It's an accumulation of the experiences one might go through. I am not even claiming that these are my personal experiences. I somehow wrote the lines as they came to me. I believe art should be as free as the air. Even its light presence can sustain the living.

Thanks for reading this. I hope you enjoy the stories I have shared in the form of poems.

Thanks & Regards,
Piyush

Her

How old were you?
When the sky just fell down on you
Barely 14?
But even the god didn't try to spare you
All the fires came and went,
You pretended that nothing ever happened
But ashes still remained,
How could you smile so brightly?
"I don't feel a thing," you always said it
But your eyes tell me everything lately,
I wish if I could turn back time,
I wish if I could do something right,
I wish if I could rinse those scars off you
I wish if I could take that pain from you
I just wish
Whatever that is yours belongs to me now

Leave all the pressure on me; I am too
strong
It's time for you to get freed now
Our journey is hard and the road is long,
But don't you worry. I got your back now,
Daddy's little Angel you are,
Those wings are not a show-off
You have to fly far,
And when you would be in that free sky,
Don't you fear for falling down,
Just know that I would be right there for
you,
Right there to catch you,
Even when the Gods turn against us,
I will be there for you
Nothing can ever try to ruin that smile of
yours now,
You have gone through a lot,
It used to be hell, right?
I would make it a heaven for you

Skirmish Within

He came home early to find her already in
bed,
One more day has gone by without a word
being said,
It's already March end and work pressure is
actually killing him,
He thinks, "Am I that cursed? Am I that
sinned?"
His fingertips keep calculating the money,
He chuckles helplessly and wonders what's
so funny,
Endless needs and limited incomes,
Expenses are building a mountain and there
is no rise in a penny,
His heart dies every day,
Just for two more words to say,
He keeps ruining his nights

To make others' day.
Every move he took led him to fail,
Every axe is indeed carved for a tree to
break,
They talk about being stronger,
But nothing is stronger than a man
rebuilding himself.

The Big Brother

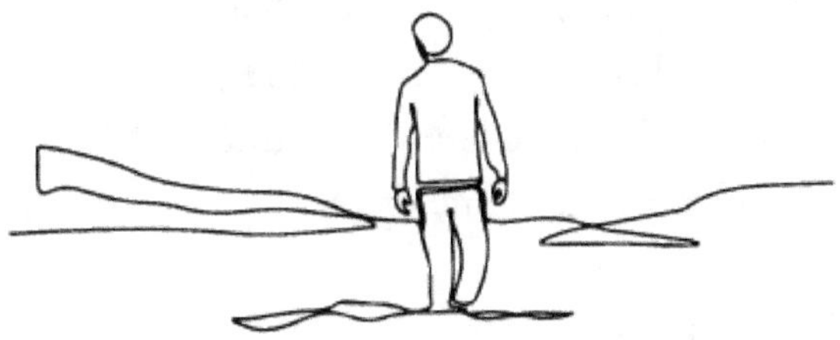

He is so happy to hear that he has become a
big brother,
Three-year-old is carrying now the unknown
responsibilities on his own shoulders,
They say that a mother never parts her love
among her children,
Then 3-year-old questions why mother loves
his younger brother more,
It's very comparative between the two now,
Questions are filling his head but he still
loves the little baby,
He couldn't say the reason why he is so
sanguine,
Maturity seems pretty easy for him,
Mother used to walk him to school before,
Now he explains to himself the absence of
his mother by holding his own chin, but for
what?
He deserves more pampering,

He is getting left out but still tries to feel
happy, staggering
Still, his mother raised a fine man,
He chuckles and says it's fine, as his mother
worries if his favorite food's little burnt,
Finishing the food, he drinks water, calming
his thirst,
Bikes! he likes a lot,
Hopes to fancy one at last,
While counting money, his dad went
stressed,
"No, I will manage, Father," one more day
& embarking on the train,
He struggles but is always happy or so to
say,
Lost in the mob but yet didn't lose the faith

Memories

Knowing your worth and having the ego
Could be the sides of the same coin,
So-called self-respect war is segregating our
worlds into hers and mine,
Found my angel, I remembered saying that,
Her funny horror stories of how witches are
cats,
I remembered laughing at her when she
buried her face in my chest while watching
"The Nun,"
With her, those long drives and passing time
were fun,
I remembered we were meeting after so
long,

She just came running at me, hugging me,
backed by a love song,
I remembered running my hands on her
body,
I remembered how she held me tight and
locked her lips on mine, talking
My poems don't mean anything now,
It was flawless but we were finding flaws,
Gathered so much hatred that you hate me
though,
Moving on wasn't an option; I will wait and
So,
I'm not broken; you understand it,
Hope my love would last and overstand it.

The Societal Masculinity

I wondered before how people could Change
so dramatically,
They were humans the other day, now just
monsters, sadly,
My Masculine side wasn't activated till this
Quarantine
So I wondered: I also enjoyed being the
monster, honestly
So all the things, I used to do them outside,
Indeed, I was free but had an ethical
limitation inside,
Now! I drink in front of her,

And just beat her up out of frustration,
Who is there to tell me what to do?
Yesterday I just threw a plate at her,
Just because she accidentally burnt the food,
"Marry me, I will keep you as a Queen," she
remembered that I said,
Now I stuffed that burnt food in her mouth
while saying
"Wash the damn plate."
So now it has become a war for her,
So what? Lioness is a lioness but only lions
have furs,
This is what I was taught,
I would never wonder that I am at my fault,
Because she is always there to be blamed,
That's why I have even charged her father
the dowry to make my claim,
What would she do, huh? It's "She"
Society raised me, distinguishing between
her and me,
Now I raised my voice and sometimes my
hand,
Why? Just to prove that I am the man,
She sheds tears and sits back,
What did she do to deserve that,
And sometimes I even wonder that she
didn't sign for this,

She expected a heaven but is stuck in a hell
so deep
I wish if I could ease her suffering,
I can't really! Cause I'm the cause if we try
reasoning,
My inner monster says that Society made
you this way & I agree,
I was raised distinguishing between her and
me

Anxiety and Depression

I think about it too now
I think about how I had lost you and lost
myself too,
Frustrating, we were already & angers help
too,
Angers help ruin things,
Those were the genuine things,
I see them clearly now,
And I think about it too now,
Can someone tell me why I am anxious all
the time?
Why am I facing a death penalty with no
crime,
My records seem clear as crystal,
But they always portrayed me while holding
a pistol,

What is wrong with the people! Why do I
think they hate me?
I am on medication with consistency but
they don't treat me,
Is that the reason I act so differently?
Isn't my anxiety taking over me
deliberately?
Do I have a life? I'm just left in this
incomprehensible world,
For me, the world can't read and I'm only
good with words,
Suffocation is being my shadow and a
friend,
It never leaves me; consequences are in
means of pain,
Sometimes it gets so heavy that I feel insects
crawling on my body,
I keep checking my blanket to see if my
siblings are making fun of me,
Though the insects are not real for sure,
Kind of relieved, but I'm afraid my siblings
never tried putting insects in my bed ever,
I see these things very often now,
I think about it too now
I envy those who sleep so freely,
A good warm sleep and nothing to worry
about,

All these things I know you wouldn't
understand,
My pride is too big and I wouldn't ask you
to lend a hand

The Broken

Everything looked so dark when I saw you,
My eyes were stuck on you & nothing was
visible past you,
Those glittering eyes of yours were calling
me so desperately,
Didn't think if it's love before,
Showing you off to the people was pushing
me towards the cause recklessly,
I thought it's pretty easy to have a soulmate
around,
I thought it was all about roaming hand in
hand in the surrounds,
Then we might have grown mature, and
things might have started to fall apart,

I thought of you as my life partner and now
the ways part,
I doubt if I ever gonna love someone like I
did you,
I understood the situation, but I needed this
guilt to undo,
Do you think that someone can take my
place in your life?
Maybe this would be possible in future but
agree with the fact that I was one of a kind,
I know you miss me
I know you want to kiss me,
Nobody can do a thing like you do
When you used to seduce me,
Your eyes still haunt me in my soleness,
I dream only about you, even in my
wakefulness,
At least give me a false hope that we would
be together,
Tell me, how would it feel to watch a
peacock without feathers?
They say everyone has a preset goal to meet
their soulmate,
Now I am just a dark night, as you were my
only Sun and it already had been set

Demon in Man

She raised her voice and said,
Why did he rescue her from burning flames?
A barn along with a family was moving
ahead to unite with ashes,
He was passing by and saved the girl from
the wheat plains,
His alter ego was laying eyes on the
helpless,
By bringing his superiority in the games,
He snatched an alive pup from its own kin,
She saw her family dissolving in the fire,
The man helped her, made her want her life
as desired,
He brought her to his home,

A nice villa situated near the shore,
He treated her nicely, putting a cup of wine
in front of her,
She drank it, as it was the only cure,
His warm smile now started comforting her,
His hands started folding into greeting ones,
She wondered why the God like him
embraced her life this late,
Maybe she hadn't had a clue of her
unfortunate fate,
He came closer to her the other night,
He held her untouched body by anyone yet
so tight,
She felt like getting loved for the first time,
He pressed his body against her,
And it was so unnatural,
He only released her from the darkness to
make her see this inhumane structure,
The night passed and she was still holding
the haunting memory,
She saw him again folding hands in
greetings,
How does a monster turn into a man who
holds no threat?
Maybe she wasn't following the reality but
her incomprehensible fate

Mystification

Wandering in the wilderness,
Trying to find what's left behind,
You end up at the gates of doubts,
Somewhere even the Sun doesn't get to
shine,
So the lives become so grayish now,
Death wish is not also that kind,
Feels like you had everything a minute ago,
Now everything is taken away,
Maybe that's why things are ephemeral,
Everything is created out of clay,
Before leaving for the wilderness, you made
a truce with your own self
They did try to pull you out of gray,
But your stubborn soul wouldn't undo the
regret

The River and The Sea

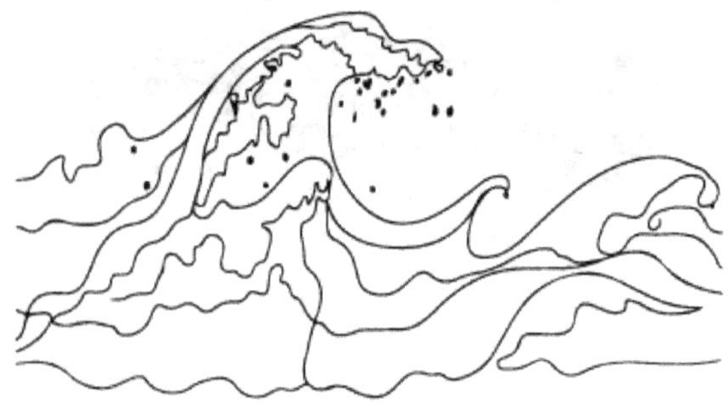

I don't know why I didn't try?
I wish you were there for one last time.
Loving someone and not getting a hug was a
big thing,
I felt like I dug so deep but stopped before
reaching the clean sweep.
How would I know that there was a mine of
diamonds on the other side of the wall?
I have waited for three years to get a call.
I waited for so long, thinking it to be true,
I literally craved for one tall girl, thinking
that I wouldn't have to lose my pride while
kissing you,
Your eyes would directly reach mine if I
held you close,
I would not have to lower the gaze to stare
into your eyes in the flow,

Our vibe might be matching so hard that we
always end up at each other's doors,
While meeting with the sea, the rivers also
change their flows,
This river of ours is now changing her flow
according to the sea she is meeting.
I might say, "I love you," but the other
words would be like, "I am just kidding"
My mind wouldn't let me accept the fact that
I am still in love with you,
The more I try to go back to my place but
what could I do?
It's nature; every thirty days, the sea has to
go deep into the river too.
Holding your hand and not letting it go
would be the dream.
But the next 30th day, the sea again would
withdraw from the river stream.
You are as beautiful as a river,
Beautiful, flowing, and for me a reviver
And I am the sea
I might look calm but that's not the part,
I'm so deep as hell filled with filth and
sharks,
My deeps were never to be counted,
The tides are never to be taunted,
I swear I love you as deep as the sea,

But some parts of me are clearly Haunted,
It's about us, the River and the Sea,
The time you would enter me, you would
want to flee,
That's why this relation is of ebb and flow,
We might love each other for a day
But rotation would cause us to lose the
close,
I would return back to the sea; you would
return back to the river,
Water would be there, but the amalgamation
of us would be never.

Agony

It does hurt so much now that I can't take it,
Looking at her photo at 3 am,
I am done being strong that I can't fake it,
Seeing that I don't have any claim,
Alcohol comes and shatters my life into
pieces,
It's 9/11 once again,
The twin towers are between my chest,
It hurts so hard; I won't wish it on even my
enemies, I swear,
Love and attachment come at a cost, so
falling in love? I won't dare,
How can I express my feelings when I really
wasn't taught to,

All I can tell is that it's like someone's
putting a knife in an already live wound,
A thousand nails going in one by one,
God, please save me this time; I want none.
None of your attractive dolls; I learnt my
lesson,
Femininity is a blessing, in my case a curse,
I completely forget her when my mind is
occupied,
When I am alone, she comes back slowly
and my heart gets sliced,
What should I do to undo this, tell me?
God, I thought I was your favorite boy when
you sent her to me,
Do you really exist? I question your
existence,
Prove it and please accept my penance,
I learnt my lesson, God. Please make this go
away,
They said tears make it go away.
Have some dignity and give me my tears to
shed,
Why you made me like this?
Like an Iron within?
God, if you have a heart, You will also cry
having seen,

I'm so broken that sometimes I can't
breathe,
Science calls it panic attacks,
But I believe it's all your will,
I learnt my lesson, God.
Please let me go,
You stripped me of everything; now what's
left?
They told me you are all father!
A father trying to kill one of his sons—what
a deft!

Avarice

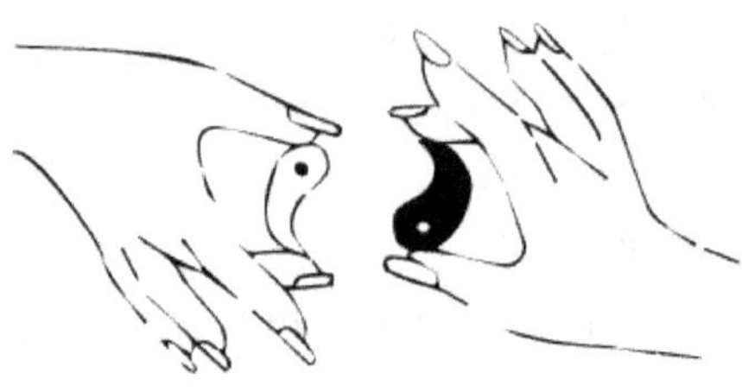

A strong young man, a strong believer,
Man of ethics and equally clever,
He believed in sacred texts and followed
them undoubtedly,
He used to counsel the people to earn the
penny,
Base of his wisdom was indeed the Holy
Bible,
The young mind was the greatest and
tackling the obstacles,
His village was small and people were few,
The Demon of greed and boasting was
taking over him and he didn't have a clue,
He decided to leave the village and go to the
city to earn more,
Sweet was his taste; now he had to deal with
the sour,
The village boy was curious about the city
life,

He didn't know the city could wrong even
the right,
A pair of clothes and the Holy Bible were
what he had,
Dark clouds were hovering over him & he
was being sad,
He thought how much he had wasted in the
village,
City didn't let him sleep; his eyes were on
the prostitute's cleavage,
Then he started drinking some booze,
His grip on the god getting loose,
Thousands of lives he might have saved
before,
Black dogs were preying on a white wolf,
His thoughts were so black that he wanted to
get laid more and more,
Forgot his prayers and forgot his chores,
The man of God denied the god himself,
Earthly lusts were weighing more than the
wisdom on the shelf,
Bugs started eating the pages of sacred texts
slowly,
The divinity had taken its hand off his head
probably,
Five years later, he might have had caught
some disease,

Incurable one and now even the prostitutes
didn't offer him anything,
Humans deny him and left him to rot,
Last drop of blood in his body, rest are the
clots,
How lust and greed can be the great regrets,
What a strong character he was! Now just a
rotten book of secrets!

The God

Every creation has a creator, they say,
Earth is nothing but a god's play,
The angels pull the strings and make you do
what you do,
Free will is yours, then angels are whom you
are about to sue,
I don't understand the religion, I must say,
God created humans out of clay?
All these religious books seem rubbish
sometimes,
Angels pulling the strings and there is an
increase in crimes,
Humans committing atrocities against
humans in the name of god,

Then I feel religion is the biggest fraud,
How could you explain to me the rape of a
3-month-old child,
Angels and strings are not godly but wild,
I think maybe angels are true controllers and
god's grip is too mild,
Humans commit the worst of the things and
still whine,
Where is this world headed, can you
specify?
It will be too late for god too if he tries to
rectify

Sentience

What has happened to me?
I wish I would have known
I think I lost it all while just trying to be free
Life became so dependent on the dreams,
once I was shown,
Now I'm literally killing it, can say on a
killing spree,
But seems like I was pierced by the blade I
had honed
It's totally okay to be sad, I see
Nothing can satisfy the need of constantly
not being home,
I might have earned the fortune wealth-wise,
Money is piling up, but at what price?
Being independent and dependent are the
sides of the same coin,

I feel like I have a lot of fancy words but
lost the voice,
Pretended to become a lot of things, making
myself a fool,
Cigarettes, alcohol, and sometimes may be
an extremist, just to be cool,
Time keeps calculating things at its own
pace,
Feels like it's just me, "someone I hate," and
a lot of empty space

Misery

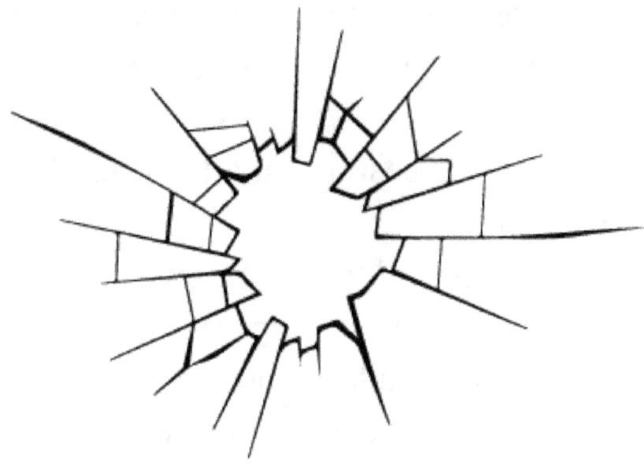

They were fighting so hard that day,
I got afraid and hid under the bed,
I heard a scream followed by a body
thudding,
Next morning, they said she got silent
forever,
They also didn't let me see my father there,
In school, everyone was talking about it,
Nobody knew my existence before,
Suddenly I was known after my father's
readmit,
Teachers said my father was a bad man,
They said that he smashed my mother's
head with a beer can,
I didn't see either of them though,

I was just afraid that day to even step on the
floor,
I had hidden my legs in the blanket that day,
I think my mother didn't really have the
money to pay,
He used to stop beating her after he used to
get the money,
He didn't stop until the last penny,
The quarrel used to last longer,
That day, it was quite shorter,
Relatives have started visiting me very often
now,
They have been kind to me somehow,
I don't understand the workings of the
world,
It's hard to assume something is a roof when
it's nothing but dark clouds.

Love

For me, well, that nectar of love was literally
over
So I'm not really peeking at any windows,
Life has been kind of stagnant but I believe
it's moving slower,
"Life is so beautiful," I heard her say,
Didn't understand a thing but my heart said
obey,
I have never seen her but feels like I know
her,
A cute little fox but immensely clever,
My unresting mind keeps telling me stories
about her,
I have seen roses and lotuses but she seems
a sunflower,
Unending thoughts with limited information,
When she is around, I feel like I am on
vacation,

I can't take my eyes off her beautiful face,
Even when is she not around, it's only her
for my heart to chase,
I sense happiness whenever she goes,
I want to walk on her path, retracing her
every step

Adverse

You always showed me your worst,
They doubt if there was anything except
lust,
Time was so limited and less,
But there was a lot about you for me to
learn,
I was told that you weren't the one for me,
But it was you with whom I felt so lively,
I have never felt this happy when I was with
you,
I would have crossed the seven seas to come
and kiss you,
Your eyes are so talkative and they convey
everything,

Don't bother about the world, as long as I
am your "King,"
And you are my "Queen" for seven lives,
I can't explain your greatness, Love.
Not even with a billion rhymes,
These words are just a little bit of what I
want to express,
You are the love of my life; don't let them
suppress,
I thought I could never love again but you
made me love you somehow,
I keep going deeper in love with you and I
don't know how,
Do not really worry about those flaws; I
have already accepted you from my core,
Let's show off our love to the world, I see
their gazes getting lowered
I want you to be here,
Forget the world and be my "forever."

Friends

We grew up so fast,
My brothers and I,
Weren't bound by blood,
But nothing less than that,
School, high school, college, and then job,
I must agree that time does fly,
I remember my brothers by my side,
When I got injured in the sport,
I remember my brothers by my side,
When I picked a fight,
I remember my brothers by my side,
When she left,
I remember my brothers by my side,
When we won the world,
Through thick and thin,

Seeing them, I realize my life is a clean sweep,
Those long video game nights,
Those parties with dim lights,
The debates, that never finish,
The fun, that never diminishes,
I remember all of it now,
I wish to live it again and again on a loop somehow,
We are growing so fast, to be honest,
I don't know how many days we have left,
I wish my brothers the luck of all time,
The unending fortune and the hand of the divine,
I'm lucky to have friends whom I can call brothers,
The ones I can call when the dark clouds hover over,
The brothers I have made for life,
Branches of the tree with a single spine

Severance

You never understand
You never understand the way I look at you,
You never understand the songs I dedicate to
you,
Life is being a little hard these days,
Where the sky above me is falling at me
straight,
The game is going out of my hands and my
soul is a bait,
I wish I could redo stuff,
Why should I redo?
If the price is again you?
Why would I wish for something like that?
Without you, I can sense me being sad,

I am so attached to you that I cannot say that
I can live without you,
But wait, you are not oxygen, so my mind
says
That I would manage without you,
It's so hard for me to bring it up,
Your love is like a poison for me, which I
drink up,
I hope you would understand someday,
I did not do anything unfair,
I really loved you and wished you the best,
I should have told this before but I was
obsessed,
Now the water is crystal clear,
I am the cold and you are the fire,
Our amalgamation would bring nothing but
steam,
I agree there is happiness but along with
three things,
The anger, the fights, and the scream

Moving On

I think I'm in disguise,
When I think about you,
I think I'm in a situation,
When I think about you
You left just like that?
I get hurt every time I think about you
I remember your lips resting on mine,
I remember your hips attracting me just fine,
Your eyes were so lustrous,
I realize these sips I took of a fine wine,
I am not sure if I could feel that ever again,
I can't forget the warmth of your body, you
lied on me then,
I remember your fragile neck with a golden
chain,

I remember placing my lips on it and it used
to drive you insane,
Pain is all that is left now with me,
I wish if I could embrace you one last time,
maybe,
These skies above me seem to have turned
shady,
No rainbows, just seasons have become
rainy,
I don't understand how to move on,
Your memories are all that I have
You might have gone already but I can't
even mourn

The End

And the day comes when everything goes
right,
You come forth and happiness that only
shines,
Things turned out to be so good that you
assume it to be reality,
But then you just wake up, out of it
And then nights go sleepless, and you say,
"You are just fine."

www.ingramcontent.com/pod-product-compliance
Lightning Source LLC
La Vergne TN
LVHW051233200726
843510LV00011B/1566